That Precious Strand of Jewishness that Challenges Authority

Five Leaves Bookshop Occasional Papers

The Current Status of Jerusalem by Edward Said
978-1-910170-09-0, 32 pages, £4

Doctor Who and the Communist: Malcolm Hulke and his career in television by Michael Herbert
978-1-910170-08-3, 32 pages, £4

Strengthening Democracy in Post-conflict Northern Ireland by Maria Power
978-1-910170-16-8, 32 pages, £4

Anarchy 38: Nottingham by Freedom Press
978-1-910170-18-2, 32 pages, £4

How We Live and How We Might Live by William Morris
978-1-910170-26-7, 28 pages, £4

Harper Lee and the American South by Katie Hamilton
978-1-910170-27-4, 28 pages, £4

That Precious Strand of Jewishness that Challenges Authority by Leon Rosselson
978-1-910170-33-5, 28 pages, £4

Available from Five Leaves or from other bookshops worldwide.
All prices include UK postage if ordered direct from
Five Leaves Bookshop.

www.fiveleavesbookshop.co.uk

That Precious Strand of Jewishness that Challenges Authority

Leon Rosselson

Five Leaves Bookshop Occasional Papers

That Precious Strand of Jewishness that Challenges Authority
by Leon Rosselson

Published in 2016 by Five Leaves Bookshop
14a Long Row, Nottingham NG1 2DH
www.fiveleavesbookshop.co.uk

Five Leaves Bookshop Occasional Paper 7
ISBN: 978-1-910170-33-5

This essay was originally presented as the 2015 Yerushah Lecture
at the Faculty of Divinity, University of Cambridge
at the invitation of Dr Daniel Weiss, to whom thanks are given

Cover image: Leon Rosselson singing 'They Said' at Zochrot's
commemoration of Deir Yassin in 2005

Designed and typeset by Five Leaves Bookshop

Printed by Russell Press in Nottingham, UK

That Precious Strand of Jewishness that Challenges Authority

This essay had its origins in the annual Yerushah Lecture at the Faculty of Divinity, University of Cambridge which I gave in March 2015. Though 'lecture' may be too grand a word for what I'd prefer to see as a conversation; or a story centred on the question of Jewish identity. Specifically my Jewish identity. And it is a question. Not just for me but for many thousands of other Jews who share my experience.

Look at it this way. Over three generations, the Jewish identity in my family has faded like an old photograph; a palimpsest from which the old writing has been erased but on which the new is as yet only faintly inscribed. I have a photo of my Yiddish-speaking grandparents, my father's parents. He was a rabbi, she was so religious she divorced her first husband for smoking on the Sabbath. They lived in a small town, a *shtetl*, in the Pale of Lithuania, oppressed by Tsarist law and anti-semitic prejudice. Of course, their Jewish identity was not in question. Nor was it for my parents.

My father came to England when he was fourteen, in 1914, to live with his uncle, Rabbi Newman, in Leicester. Yiddish was his first language, religion and music were all he knew. When he'd educated himself he became almost aggressively secular, yet having been immersed in the Torah and the Talmud and the rituals, it was still part of his being. When he stopped being a professional violinist, he became choirmaster in Willesden Green and other synagogues. I sometimes played the organ when he was conducting the choir and was surprised at how he, atheist and humanist, seemed, unlike me, so completely at home there, even if he did sometimes bring his sandwiches in on Yom Kippur, the Day of Atonement when all even slightly religious Jews fast. I have at home a manuscript he passed on to me just before he died: a life's work, his own history of the Jewish people, from earliest times to the triumph of Christianity.

My mother, born in Gomel, Belarus, was brought up in Whitechapel, with Yiddish as a background language, a vibrant Yiddish cultural life, a Jewish social life centred on the Workers' Circle, a hotbed of radical politics, and with the ever present fear of anti-semitism.

But what Jewish legacy have they left me?

In the 1947 film *Gentleman's Agreement*, about anti-semitism in America, a Jewish scientist, bearing a certain resemblance to Einstein, explains why he is considering divesting himself of his Jewish identity. 'I have no religion,' he says, 'so I'm not Jewish by religion. Science tells me that I'm not Jewish by race since there is no such thing as a distinct Jewish race. There's not even such a thing as a Jewish type.' So, he says, he will go forth and state that he is not Jewish. Then he asks himself why so many non-religious Jews still call themselves Jewish. 'Because the world makes it an advantage not to be one,' is his answer. In short, because of anti-semitism, thus confirming Sartre's argument that 'it is the anti-semite that creates the Jew'. There is no mention of the death camps in the film, nor in the other Hollywood film of the time that deals with anti-semitism, *Crossfire*.

Since then a state that calls itself Jewish has established itself and the Holocaust has, over the decades, and certainly by the end of the 1960s, moved centre stage in the consciousness of the Jewish community. Some Jews still say they are Jewish because of anti-semitism; rather more, I suspect, claim their Jewishness in order to say to Israel 'not in my name'. In neither case does that constitute a Jewish identity. It simply begs the question. Which remains, with a slight adjustment, as posed by the Jewish scientist in the film: if not religion, if not Zionism, what?

I could, of course, resign from the club. After all, what sort of Jew is it that escaped the tortuous rigmarole of the Bar Mitzvah and would be hard put to it to tell his Midrash from his Mishnah? The writer, Will Self, has done it. So, more controversially, has the Israeli historian Shlomo Sand in his book *How I Stopped Being a Jew*. Sand, of course, has a particular problem because in Israel, nationality is defined by ethnicity - Jewish (even though Jews are not an ethnic group), Arab or Druze, for example. Sand is Jewish because his mother was Jewish. His father was not Jewish. If it had been the other way round and his mother had been not-Jewish, he would have been an Israeli citizen but his nationality would have been Austrian. In October 2013, twenty-one Israelis asked the state to recognise their wish to be classified as Israeli nationals. Their request was turned down by the Supreme Court. This is a tribalism that defines the state, not as a state for all its citizens, but as a state for all the Jews in the world.

Sand also claims that 'there is no (Jewish) cultural baggage that is not religious'. I'm not ready to accept that. What's more, Israel and its prime ministers will continue to abduct my Jewish identity, as Netanyahu has recently done, if I don't claim it for myself. 'If I am not for myself, who will be for me?' as the saying goes. And 'if not now, when?'

Not that I'm obsessed by the question of Jewish identity. I have many other identities: male, old, songwriter, husband, father, grandfather, great grandfather, socialist with anarchist tendencies. At times in my life it has stirred barely a ripple on my consciousness. At other times, it has loomed large. As in 2002 when I was commissioned by the Wren Trust to write a song about what it means to be Jewish for a multicultural concert at the end of the Sidmouth Folk Festival. I took it to mean what it means to me to be Jewish and accepted the challenge without having any idea as to how to set about it.

I thought about the word 'Jewishness'. Of course, there's no such thing. No essence of Jewishness. What would it consist of? Chicken soup with *knedlach*? I thought of the common view that Jews are always arguing, debating, dissenting, questioning. Two Jews three opinions, so they say. On the other hand, in these times it sometimes seems more like 200,000 Jews one opinion. But I found stories of Jews refusing to allow God to intervene in rabbinical disputes. And I liked the story of the tailor arguing with God on Yom Kippur. He recounts the argument to the Berditschever Rabbi. I told God that my sins are small ones, he says. I may have kept left-over cloth or eaten in a non-Jewish house without washing my hands. But your sins, oh Lord, are big ones. You've taken babies from mothers and mothers from babies. But let's be quits. I'll forgive you if you forgive me. The Berditschever says: You let God off too lightly. You could at least have made him send down the Mashiach - the Messiah. Is there another religion where you're allowed to argue with God?

I thought of my parents' teaching that Jews should always be on the sides of the oppressed. The American academic Sara Roy writes that to her parents, who were Holocaust survivors, Judaism meant bearing witness, raging against injustice and foregoing silence. It meant compassion, tolerance and rescue. And there's this from Isaac Babel: *I am a Jew because of my unconditional solidarity with the persecuted and exterminated.*

This seemed like a promising starting point. With their history as an often persecuted minority, that ought to be true. But was it? There are universalist texts in the Torah and in the Prophets speaking truth to power and railing against injustice and the greed and arrogance of the mighty. 'Do not ill treat a stranger or oppress him for you were strangers in Egypt,' is often quoted. Or 'Execute truth, justice and peace within your gates.' There's no doubt that the Old Testament has given heart and hope to oppressed peoples, notably black slaves in America. And, interestingly, since I've written songs about both Gerrard

Winstanley and the Diggers, and Abiezer Coppe and the Ranters, both these radical groups which flourished briefly at the time of the English revolution found inspiration and solidarity over the centuries in the Jewish Bible.

When Winstanley and another Digger leader, William Everard, met with General Fairfax to explain why the Diggers had taken over the common land at St George's Hill in April 1649, Everard said that he was of the race of the Jews; that all the liberties of the people were lost by the coming in of William the Conquerer and that ever since, the people of God had lived under tyranny and oppression worse than that of our forefathers under the Egyptians. But now the time of deliverance was at hand and God would bring his people out of this slavery and restore them to their freedom in enjoying the fruits and benefits of the earth.

And Abiezer Coppe in *A Fiery Flying Roll* sounds like a 17th century Isaiah: 'If I have bread it shall or should be his else my religion is in vain. I am for dealing bread to the hungry, for clothing the naked, for the breaking of every yoke, for the letting of the oppressed go free.'

On the other hand, isn't it dangerous to base any argument on selected extracts from the Bible since in this rich mix reflecting over a thousand years of history, it would not be difficult to find evidence to prove the opposite?

Worse, it is now being used to justify a Greater Israel. So while there may be a universalist strand, there is also the tribal, stemming from the concept of the "chosen people", which rejoices in the slaughter of idolaters and the Egyptian first born and the destruction of the cities of the Hittites and the Amorites and the Canaanites and the Amalekites and...

In any case, with their facility for interpreting and reinterpreting, rabbis can make even the simplest commandment mean something quite different. According to the settler Rabbis Yitzhak Shapira and Yossi Elitzur in their book *Torat HaMelech*, Thou Shalt Not Kill actually applies only to Jews killing other Jews, not to gentiles.

I pondered on the fact that Jews have been disproportionately represented in revolutions and progressive causes, in radical groups fighting for justice: Mensheviks, Bolsheviks, communists, socialists, anarchists - particularly anarchists. Think of Emma Goldman, Alexander Berkman, Noam Chomsky, Abby Hoffman, Alan Ginsberg, Howard Zinn, Murray Bookchin, Erich Fromm. The Yiddish-speaking peoples of Eastern Europe gave birth to the socialist Bund seeking a transformation of society to the benefit of all but wanting to keep their own Jewish identity, culture, language; and also to anarchist groups, anarchist newspapers, anarchist ideas that immigrants to Britain and America brought with them. Is this because of the freethinking tradition in Judaism that questions authority and allows you to argue with God?

In apartheid South Africa, according to Gillian Slovo, the great majority of whites who refused to close their eyes to the injustices of apartheid were Jews, including her parents, Joe Slovo and Ruth First. Jews were also strongly represented in the Civil Rights movement in the States, New York rabbis thundering their condemnation of segregation based on the text: *Justice, justice, you shall pursue.*

On the other hand, the Jewish communities in the Southern States, shopkeepers and merchants in the thriving cotton industry, though they did not strive to preserve segregation, didn't speak out against it either. Whatever instincts for justice they may have derived from their religion or their history were trumped by their class interests. As usually happens.

In South. Africa, too, the Jewish mainstream comfortably accommodated itself to power and the privileges of their whiteness. The South African Board of Deputies, the representative body of South African Jewry, didn't condemn apartheid until 1985.

The story is the same in Britain. While many Jews were active in the Communist Party, in working class struggles against greedy landlords and exploitative employers, in the fight against fascism in London and in Spain, the concerns of the representatives of mainstream Jewry, the British Board of Deputies, the *Jewish Chronicle*, were — and largely still are — tribal. Transformation of society is not on their agenda. What motivates them is their desire to be accepted and to this end loyalty to the state is paramount and troublemaking is discouraged. 'Stay off the streets' was the Board's advice while thousands of Jews were gathering to stop Mosley's Fascists marching through the East End. In these times it seems more like loyalty to two states; a matter of singing *Hatikvah*, the Israeli national anthem, and toasting the Queen.

So what am I to conclude from these games of on the one hand, on the other hand? That there is a tribal Jewish identity certainly; one that asks the joke question, Is it good for the Jews? And responds to the Holocaust with the demand: never again must this happen to the Jews. 'If I am not for myself, who will be for me?' Yes. But there is a universalist one, too, that asserts never again for anyone, that sees in its own suffering, the suffering of others and that seeks its own emancipation in the emancipation of all. 'If I am for myself alone, what am I?' to complete Rabbi Hillel's aphorism.

I had, I thought, a way into the song I'd been asked to write and an answer to the question: what - for me - does it mean to be Jewish? The problem then was to turn this into a song. Because a song is not - or should not be - an abstraction, a generalisation, a declaration or an argument. It is a story about people. I could only make the song work by basing it on the life and beliefs of my father.

My Father's Jewish World

My father came here as a boy from Tsarist Russia
From Vilkavishki in the Pale those reservations for the Jews
His schooling was the Talmud and the Torah
The writings of the rabbis and their laws
Music was his door to freedom Yiddish was his mother tongue
And home was just a dreamland in a song.

He told us stories of his gentle rabbi father
And of his mother who was fearless and the hardships that
    they faced
And when the drunken peasants got together
And yelled, Let's kill the Jews for killing Christ
His mother grabbed the rolling pin she used to make the
    Sabbath bread
And ran to crack their skulls, my father said.

It's not a nation. Not a religion
This Jewish spirit is still unbroken
It's like the candle that mocks the darkness
It's like the song that shatters the silence
It's like the fool who laughs at the dragon
It's like the spark that signals rebellion
It's like the dance that circles unending.

He lived in England half belonging half a stranger
Always feeling much as I do on the outside looking in
In time he grew to be an unbeliever
Religion had become a mental chain
Abandoned God became a Jewish atheist and then with pride
A Communist until the day he died.
So no more Bible but instead *The Daily Worker*
People came and people argued, asking questions how and
    why
Revolution, Stalin, Trotsky, Soviet Russia
Two Jews, three opinions. so they say
God loves the poor and helps the rich, the Jewish father tells
    his son
And so you've got to choose which side you're on.

It's not a nation....

He read the books of Jewish rebels like Spinoza
And he sang songs that laughed at rabbis in a language that's
    not mine
He loved the Yiddish stories and their humour
The humour born from poverty and pain
Sleep faster for we need the pillows - how else could the Jews
    survive
And keep their tattered dreams and hopes alive?
But now my father's Jewish world has gone forever
Burned in the flames of hatred, nothing left but ash & dust
And Yiddish lingers on out of nostalgia
How can I make some meaning from what's past?
And the state they say is Jewish carved from stolen land brings
    only shame
By torturing and killing in our name.

It's not a nation....

Now it's my father's face that meets me in the mirror
And I wonder what to me his Jewish legacy has been
The state of always being an outsider
Of asking why then asking why again
That precious strand of Jewishness that challenges authority
And dares to stand against the powers that be.
Emma Goldman, Rosa Luxembourg, Bar Kochba
The Jewish anarchists and socialists who fought to free the poor
The ones who meet injustices with anger
And will not let their dreams drown in despair
Who speak up for the refugees, defend the weak against the
    strong
It's for these rebel Jews I sing my song.

It's not a nation....

***

I remember the 1947, 1948 war in Palestine. It's the only time I've had anti-semitic abuse aimed at me because the terrorist groups, Irgun and the Stern gang, were hanging and shooting British soldiers, bombing hotels, assassinating diplomats and planting bombs in the Foreign and Colonial Office in London. My Communist Party parents were broadly supportive of the Jewish state because of the Holocaust but also because the Soviet Union supported the Partition Plan and Communist Czechoslovakia sent arms to the Haganah, the Jewish underground army. Of course we knew nothing of the massacres, the Death March, Plan Dalet, which resulted in the forcible expulsions of the indigenous people, nor would we for decades to come. Israel's war against the Arabs was seen entirely through the lens of the Zionist narrative.

In my early teens, I joined Hashomer Hatzair, the Young Guard, the youth movement of Mapam which defined itself as Socialist Zionist at a time when that didn't seem like an impossible contradiction. The movement sent over *shlichim* — "messengers" — leaders whose job it was to persuade us that we should all make *aliyah* — "ascent" — thus rising up from our low, money-fixated, abnormal lives as diaspora Jews into the exalted idealistic life in *Eretz Israel*, preferably on a Kibbutz. According to the movement's pseudo-Marxist analysis, Jewish society was like an upside-down pyramid, a small working class base supporting a preponderance of the intelligentsia and the moneyed classes. Only in a state of their own, in Palestine, could the pyramid be turned the right way up so that Jews could lead normal lives and engage in the class struggle alongside the Arab proletariat, whose interests they shared. Or so they said. Yiddish, the language of my father, was disparaged as the language of the ghetto Jew who, so the myth has it, went meekly into the gas chambers.

Chazak ve'ematz they told us: be strong and courageous. Israel was giving birth to the new pioneering Jew, Hebrew-speaking, healthy, sturdy, outdoor, self-confident, virtues brilliantly exemplified by our born-in-Palestine teachers, Sabras, who were indeed all of those things. I was impressed by the vision they offered. The only problem I had was that I couldn't see anything Jewish about these *chazak ve'ematz* Israelis. And I really liked the sound of my father's Yiddish and the songs he sang. So would I have to leave all that behind and sing instead Hebrew songs about marching south to Eilat and making the desert bloom like a rose?

Afterwards I realised that we'd actually been guided towards this Zionist ideology quite gently compared to, say, the account of Uri Avnery, the ex-Irgun now peace campaigner and writer. 'In the Zionist school in Palestine,' he writes, 'we were taught that the essence of Zionism is the negation of the Diaspora (called exile in Hebrew). Not just the physical negation but the mental too. Not only the demand that every single Jew come to the land of Israel but also the total repudiation of all forms of Jewish life in Exile: their culture and their language, Yiddish. The absolutely worst thing we could say about anybody was to call him an Exile Jew. Herzl's writings exude in places a strongly anti-Semitic odour.' Indeed they do. And Zionism and anti-Semitism look like two sides of the same coin.

Isaac Deutscher recounts a conversation he had with Ben Gurion in the 1950s about non-Zionist Jews. 'They have no roots,' Ben Gurion said. 'They are rootless cosmopolitans - there can be nothing worse than that.' 'Rootless cosmopolitans' is the accusation made against Jews by Stalin and his followers.

And, of course, nationalists see it as a defect that could be dangerous. I see it as a virtue, a gift. Living on the edge of society, not quite belonging, on the outside looking in, as the song says, can give Jews a vantage point from which to view society sceptically, questioningly, critically, making them less susceptible to the crude appeals of patriotism. Reflecting on my experience in Hashomer led me to the conclusion that whatever the answer is to the question of my Jewish identity, it isn't Zionism, it isn't Israel.

But I did go to Israel in 1958. I'd finished a stint playing the accordion in a play called *The Hamlet of Stepney Green* by the

Jewish writer Bernard Kops directed by the Jewish director Frank Hauser who, irritatingly, used to address me as *boychik*. You see how Jewish identity follows you around even when you don't want it to, dancing along behind like a wilful child — *look at me, look at me*. So when an Israeli singer, Zimra Ornatt, for whose Topic record I'd provided guitar accompaniments asked me to work with her in Israel, I thought I might as well.

I've never felt more English than in the year I spent in Israel. Being British was an advantage as Western Jews ranked highly in the hierarchy that made up Israeli society - Sabras securely established at the top, Jews from North Africa and the Arab countries bumping along at the bottom. I was shocked to hear, on Kibbutz Zikim, the Israeli wife of a friend in Hashomer call them *shachorim*. Blacks. If their language was Arabic, that was even more shameful because speaking Arabic was worse than speaking Yiddish. Palestinians, of course, then living under military administration, didn't figure at all in the discourse. Ten years later Golda Meir was still assuring us that there were no such people as Palestinians.

So, being English I was assigned to the best *ulpan* — the school where new immigrants were taught Hebrew. A young Mizrachi (Middle Eastern Jewish) woman from Aleppo in Syria and then Beirut was sent to a low-grade overcrowded *ulpan* until, French-speaking, she redefined herself as from Paris and ascended to the best *ulpan*. Which was fortunate because that's where we met and that's how we later got married.

I spent a lot of time in The Last Chance, a nightclub in Beersheva run by a French woman, Betty Knut, who happened to be the terrorist who'd planted the bomb in the Foreign and Colonial Office in London on behalf of the Stern Gang. A rich diversity of Jews from different countries with different cultures, identities and languages gathered there. In 1982 I wrote a *songspiel* called 'The Last Chance' about my experience there. It centred on an argument between two characters who frequented the place, Sam, a Yiddish-speaking immigrant from France and Meier, a nationalistic Israeli. At one point, Sam asks, 'We are Jews. Why should our children turn into Israelis?' To which Meier replies: 'History loves a winner. No more guilt, no more fear, no more being strangers, no more being different.' Sam insists: 'I like being different. I want to be different.' But Meier saw the future. This rich diversity of Jewish peoples would one day merge into one homogeneous Hebrew-speaking Israeliness. And wasn't that sad? And if the Zionist demand that all Jews everywhere move to Israel was implemented, wouldn't that be a shocking end to 4000 years of Jewish history? And a tragic loss to the countries in which Jews have lived and to which they have made their contribution.

The other divide I found on my stay in Israel was between the secular and the religious. All the secular Israelis I mixed with considered themselves as Israeli first and Jewish a long way behind, if at all. For them Jewishness meant first and foremost the religion and they resented their freedoms being restricted by the power religion had in civil affairs. No marriage or divorce without the rabbis' consent, no public transport on *Shabbat* in many cities. The Orthodox and Ultra-Orthodox predicted then that they would prevail. 'We have children,' they said. 'They - the liberal Israelis - have cats.' Their prediction, as it turns out, was correct.

The Six Day War in 1967 was a turning point for me and, I believe, for many others. It became increasingly clear that the trajectory Israel was taking - military aggression, expansion, facts on the round, discrimination against its non-Jewish citizens - was not a deviation from Zionism; it *was* Zionism. Over the decades the Zionist narrative unravelled, starting with the myths around the Six Day War itself. And the narrative of 'the other' made itself heard for those willing to listen without prejudice. The Holocaust became much more prominent in Zionist discourse after the Six Day War, often used as a justification for Israel's hard-line policies. It could no longer be seriously argued that Israel, one of the most militarised states in the world, with nuclear weapons and the most sophisticated military technology supplied by its American ally, was the little David surrounded by hostile Goliaths ready to throw all the Jews into the sea.

In winter 1992, during the first, non-violent intifada, I watched on TV a group of four hundred Hamas leaders shivering on a Lebanese mountain. They had been exiled there by the Rabin government. This must have made a great impression on me because there's a reference to it in a song I wrote in 1995 called 'The Song of Martin Fontasch'. The story comes from Primo Levi's book about Jewish partisans in the Second World War, *If Not Now When?* Martin Fontasch is a poet, songwriter, carpenter who is given one last chance to write a song before the Nazis execute him. The song he writes is about standing up for yourself, taking its cue from the first half of the saying attributed to Rabbi Hillel: 'If I am not for myself, who will be? If not now when?' I thought that had he survived, like Sara Roy's parents, he would have written a different sort of song, one that draws on the second half of that saying: 'If I am for myself alone, what am I?'

The Song of Martin Fontasch

The story's told of how in 1942
Martin Fontasch, poet, carpenter and Jew
With a band of partisans threw in his lot
Till he was taken by the Germans to be shot.
He was a peaceful man, quick to laugh and cry
At every village celebration he'd be there
With his songs that told of sadness and of joy
And the guitar he carried with him everywhere
But when the Nazis came and killed his wife and son
Martin traded his guitar in for a gun.

And this song is for those who are cast out by history
The banned and abandoned the spurned and ignored
Whose homes have been taken whose dreams have been
     broken
Who huddled on hillsides demand to be heard.

The German soldier assigned to kill the Jew
As it happened was a music lover too
And this bond, it seems, is what made him decide
To offer Martin one last wish before he died
Soon my soul, Martin said, will dance on air
Now all I ask is time to write my farewell song
The German soldier checked his watch and said 'one hour'
One hour? Martin remarked, that long?
And so he wrote and sang full-voiced to wake the dead
And then the German put a bullet in his head.

And this song is...

The German kept the song and bragged of what he'd done
And showed it proudly, when in drink, to everyone
He couldn't read the words and didn't seem to see
That a song can not take root unless it's free
And then one night two partisans set out
The song must be released, the man must die
They slipped into his quarters slit his throat
Took back the song and gave it wings to fly
And so it soared upon the wind and came to rest
And found a home among the damned and dispossessed.

And his song was ....

Though we resist oppression still our dream is peace
Theirs is the mask of hatred, ours the human face

Then let not our sufferings turn our souls to ice
So that we do to strangers what was done to us.
It is not with conquering armies I belong
Their bloody retribution I disown
Their songs of triumph I will never sing
For the God they worship turns them into stone.
If any teach their children how to hate and hurt
Though they are Jews they do not live inside my heart.

And his song is...

Let his song be a spark, let it fly through the dark
Like a bird

***

In April 2005, I went with a group, some Jewish, some not, to the West Bank to see for myself what life was like for Palestinians living under military occupation. We went to the Bethlehem area, East Jerusalem, Nablus, Ramallah, a village called Budrus and various checkpoints and roadblocks in between. We returned depressed and distressed at what we had witnessed.

I don't want to talk about the wall, the checkpoints, the settlements, the house demolitions, the settler roads and all the paraphernalia of occupation. I just want to recount a few experiences that touch on Jewish identity. On 7 April we join a demonstration of about 150 Jews and non-Jews in the religious Jewish Har Nof district of Jerusalem within sight of Yad Vashem, the major Holocaust Museum, to commemorate the notorious massacre in the Palestinian village of Deir Yassin in April 1948. It is organised by an Israeli group called Zochrot - remembering - which tries to remind Israelis of the narrative of the other, specifically the Palestinian catastrophe, the Nakba. Most Israelis prefer not to remember or are in denial. But unless Israel acknowledges the Nakba, there can be no understanding between the two peoples. Deir Yassin no longer exists. A mental hospital has been built on the site. There are songs and speeches. An eighty year-old woman recounts her story of how she survived the massacre. A group of Orthodox kids in their *yarmulkas* watch wonderingly. They chatter, they shout, they laugh. Under instructions from an adult, they tear up the pamphlets that are being handed out, 'Remember Deir Yassin'.

Isn't remembering a sacred Jewish duty? Doesn't the Torah many times commend Jews to remember? Is it only our suffering we must remember or is it all crimes, including those we commit against others? Har Nof, you may remember, is where the killings in the synagogue took place in November 2014. Israel has now criminalised commemoration of the Nakba. So it goes.

Many Palestinians, maybe most Palestinians, refer to Israelis as 'the Jews'. Not surprising given the insistence on the Jewishness of the state (it wasn't so in the 50s when I was there).

In a Palestinian cafe in East Jerusalem the woman proprietor is complaining that her son, who lives on the Mount of Olives, is being prevented from visiting her. But they are allowing 'the Jews' in, she says. This upsets me. I'm being implicated in Israel's actions. They're not Jews, I want to say. They're Israelis. I want to tell her that I'm Jewish and I'm opposed to Israel's policies. But perhaps this isn't the time. There's a lot of tension and anger about on this day. A group of religious settlers are threatening to invade Temple Mount and Palestinian men are being stopped from entering the mosque to pray.

On the Mount of Olives we can see below skirmishes involving Palestinian youths and Israeli soldiers and police. A group of angry Palestinian young men and boys are also watching. One of them asks me aggressively, 'Are you Jewish?' 'We're British,' I reply without a moment's thought. As we make our way back past the police and demonstrators, a crowd of Palestinian youths run past. 'Go back to your homes,' one of them shouts in English. They think we're

Israelis. 'Jewish shit' another shouts in Arabic. Who do I blame for this?

We visit Budrus, a village situated between Ramallah and the Israeli border, and are welcomed by Abu Ahmed, the community leader who is coordinating the weekly non-violent protests against the barrier, here an electrified fence topped with razor wire that will cut them off from their orchards and that is destroying their precious olive trees. The fence will not only separate the village from Israel on the west side but also from Ramallah to the east, giving the lie to the assertion that Israel's security is the purpose of the Wall. As we're walking in the village, a group of children hail us. *Shalom*, they call. I'm puzzled. Why so friendly? They think you're the Israelis who come to help us, Abu Ahmed explains. Rabbis for Human Rights, Anarchists against the Wall, Ta'ayush.

It strikes me then that the hostility towards 'the Jews' is not deeply rooted in any kind of racial prejudice but is the product of this political conflict and if it was settled peacefully, if the occupation ended, if Israel became a state for all its citizens, mutual tolerance would prevail and peaceful coexistence would be possible.

Meanwhile the peaceful protests were being met with tear gas, beatings, live bullets and killings leading to more anger and hate. Olives are at the heart of Palestinian culture and their economy. Hundreds of thousands of olive trees have been destroyed by settlers and by the Israeli Defence Forces during this long occupation. Some, like those we saw in the settlement of Ma'ale Adumim, had been uprooted and brought back to Israel to be sold, as reported by the daily paper *Yediot Aharanot*. On the first night of 2015, six thousand olive saplings recently planted on Palestinian land were destroyed by settlers from an illegal outpost, Adi Ad, near Turmusaya.

As a Jew, whose side should I be on? Whose story should I be singing?

If I am for myself alone, what am I?

Song of the Olive Tree

My father's father's father planted here
In this now broken earth an olive tree
And as a child I sang to it my secrets
And as I grew I felt it part of me.
Its branches gave me shelter from the sun
Its grey green leaves shaded my young dreams
The fruit it bore was like a gift of hope
Of all the olive trees I loved this one.

The settlers came they beat us black and blue
They said, Next time we shoot you. Understand?
But still we dared to come we had no choice
We came at night like thieves to our own land.
Like ghosts we came, men, women, young and old
To pick the crop as we have always done
For centuries we harvested in peace
The oil we pressed was sweet, precious as gold.

Now look. This is a cemetery for trees.
Their great machines crushed hope into despair
They ripped the heart from every living tree
Except for one, my tree they chose to spare.
They dug it up, they smuggled it away
This ancient tree, they saw it as a prize
For some Israeli rich enough to pay
Five thousand dollars' worth, that's what they say.

Do you believe in ghosts? Last night I dreamed
My father's father's father came to me
He took my hand and held it in his own
And said, Take heart, here is my olive tree.
And when I woke it was a kind of birth

And in my hand I found an olive stone
And in the field where once my tree had been
A thousand shapes arose out of the earth.

I saw their faces, women, children, men
And each hand held a perfect olive stone
And each heart held a vision of to come
When all our olive trees will rise again.

***

In 2007 IJV, Independent Jewish Voices, was formed. I was on the steering committee. Its declaration, published in *The Times* on 5 February and in the *Jewish Chronicle* on 9 February, included this statement: "We hereby reclaim the tradition of Jewish support for universal freedoms, human rights and social justice. The lessons we have learned from our history compel us to speak out."

The hostile reaction from the mainstream Jewish community was beyond all reason, vicious, vituperative, hysterical even. Not just from the lunatic fringe like Melanie Phillips who thinks any criticism of Israel is the first step towards genocide but even from Liberal rabbis. Even the name seemed to alarm them. Independent Jewish Voices. What's not to like? It's not Jews for Justice for Palestinians. Aren't Jews supposed to be independently minded? Not it seems where Israel is concerned. IJV were accused of fostering anti-semitism, maligning Israel, of not belonging to the Jewish community and therefore having no claim to speak. Yet the Declaration is remarkably mild. There's no maligning of Israel. It simply states the case, based on Jewish history and Jewish values, for upholding human rights and international law.

There was, as I know, no uniformity of views with regard to Israel among the IJV signatories. Some were Zionist, simply wanted an end to the occupation because they believed it was corrupting the Jewish state. So why the violent response?

'The question of identity,' writes James Baldwin, 'is a question involving the most profound panic. Identity would seem to be the garment with which one covers the nakedness of the self.' It does seem as if for many Jews any criticism of Israel is an attack on their own identity leading to panic and the fear of that identity being undermined, leaving them defenceless. But can this tribal identification endure? Is support for Israel a viable Jewish identity?

The United Synagogue proclaims as one of its core values 'the centrality of Israel in Jewish life'. How can that be? In what way? And whose Jewish life? State power, in one of the most militarised states in the world with its nuclear weapons and helicopter gunships and daily violations of international law, is placed at the centre of Jewish life. Isn't that a form of idolatry?

Israel is losing support across the Diaspora. Even in America where the fastest-growing Jewish organisation is not the right wing American Israel Public Affairs Committee or the moderately progressive J Street but Jewish Voice for Peace standing on universalist Jewish principles in challenging the power of the lobby and opposing Israel's denial of Palestinian rights.

During the assault on Gaza in 2014, in London, only about 1500 could bring themselves to publicly demonstrate their support for Israel. Many who had been supportive were appalled by the slaughter of civilians, especially children, the deliberate destruction of civilian infrastructure and the vicious anti -Arab racism and dehumanisation of Palestinians that went with it. To me that assault was the ultimate betrayal of that precious strand of Jewishness that I claim as my Jewish identity, an identity I share with a growing number of Jews in the Diaspora who place solidarity with the oppressed above the demands of tribalism; and with those in Israel who dare to stand against the powers that be: journalists like Gideon Levy and Amira Hass, activists like Uri Avnery and organisations like Rabbis for Human Rights, B'tselem, Zochrot, Women in Black, Breaking the Silence, Anarchists against the Wall, Israeli Committee Against House Deomolitions and more.

I want to finish with this song which I wrote in anger and despair at the height of the assault on Gaza....

The Ballad of Rivka and Mohammed

I was watching the news from Gaza
And I closed my eyes in despair
And when I awoke from my slumber
A young girl was standing there.

She said, My name is Rivka
They killed me because I'm a Jew
I died in the ghetto of Vilna
In nineteen forty-two.

The ghetto was like a prison
They wouldn't allow us to leave
Some said they were going to kill us all
We didn't know what to believe.

That day I wore my new red dress
My *bubbe* had made for me
And in that crowded ghetto
It made me feel proud and free.

I looked up at the soldier
I looked him in the eye
I forgot to bow my head down
And so I had to die.

He smashed my head with his rifle
Because I was too bold
I was killed in the Vilna ghetto
When I was seven years old.

And then out of the darkness
A young boy's gaze met mine
He said, My name is Mohammed
My country is Palestine.

I've lived all my life in Gaza
And the only time I feel free
Is when I go down to the harbour
And feel the wind from the sea.

That day I went with my cousins
We ran down to the beach to play
Then the soldier fired a shell at me
And blew my life away.

They think they can crush our spirits
They want us to feel afraid
Locked up in the prison of Gaza
The prison that they have made.

To them our lives don't matter
They force us to live in a cage
I was killed on the beach in Gaza
At eleven years of age.

They don't think that we deserve freedom
Or belong to the human race.
Mohammed, my brother, said Rivka,
This world is a cold, cold place.

Mohammed, my friend, my brother,
Let us leave this world of war.
Then each took the hand of the other
And then they were seen no more.

But I saw spokesmen and politicians
Lining up to speechify
And every word was a hypocrite
And every word was a lie.

I saw children still being slaughtered
The monster must have its fill
While the people with power turned a blind eye
And supplied the weapons that kill.

And the people with power turn a blind eye
And enable the monster to kill.